Miranda Marquez

COVER ART BY
Anneliese Felipe

Dedicated to Leslie Snyder
INDEFATIGABLE

Bryan Lemus

Arturo Franco Monjares

Miranda Marquez

Norberto Aragon Jr.

Luis Aldo

Leonardo Lomeli

Yaretzi Hernandez

Charlie Nelson

Samuel Rodriguez

Luna Arzate

Carlos Garcia

Bella Moresi

Natalie Martinez

Edgar Bautista Mendez

Jennyfer Jimenez

Joana G.

Joana Gomez

Jason Martinez

An Awesome Bird
The Pelican

By Rusty Austin
Illustrations
The Students at
Nellie Coffman Middle School
Cathedral City, California

For The Nellie Coffman Middle School
Go Cougars!

TABLE OF ANIMALS

Pelican ...
Salmon ...
Wide Eyed Lemur ...
Scorpion ...
Roadrunner ...
Blue Footed Booby ...
Axolotl ...
Koala Bear ...
Mockingbird ...
Egyptian Uromastyx ...
Beaver ...
Trumpeter Swan ...
Two Toed Sloth ...
Kingbird ...
Coyote ...
Texas Armadillo ...
Prairie Dog ...
Falcon ...
California Condor ...
Carolina Chickadee ...
Eel ...

American Bison...
Toucan ...
Chipmunk ...
Jackrabbit ...
Nutcracker ...
Barracuda ...
Common Mole ...
Mink ...
Lynx ...
Long Tailed Weasel ...
Marmot ...
Paedophryne Amauensis ...
Caiman ...
Rainbow Trout ...
Penguin ...
Vermillion Flycatcher ...
Mollusk ...
DO IT YOURSELF
Rhinoceros ...
Duckbill Platypus ...
Ladybug ...
Tarantula ...

Julian Meza Morales

An awesome bird, The Pelican
he keeps in his beak
his food
for the week

Yaretzi Hernandez

When called upstream
The Salmon won't stop
until she makes it
TO THE TOP

Julieann Rivera

The Wide Eyed Lemur
likes to live at night
which is why
she has such wide eyes
to giver her stellar night sight

Andres Ulloa

The Scorpion packs
a mighty stinger
and you better watch out
or she'll stinger your finger

Fernando Jimenez

The Roadrunner has zygodactyl toes which means they go to and fro

Andres Ulloa

**The Blue Footed Booby
has blue feet, true
so better seen
by me and you**

Matthew Franz

**The Axolotl
can regrow his brain
which is a handy thing
for an Axolotl**

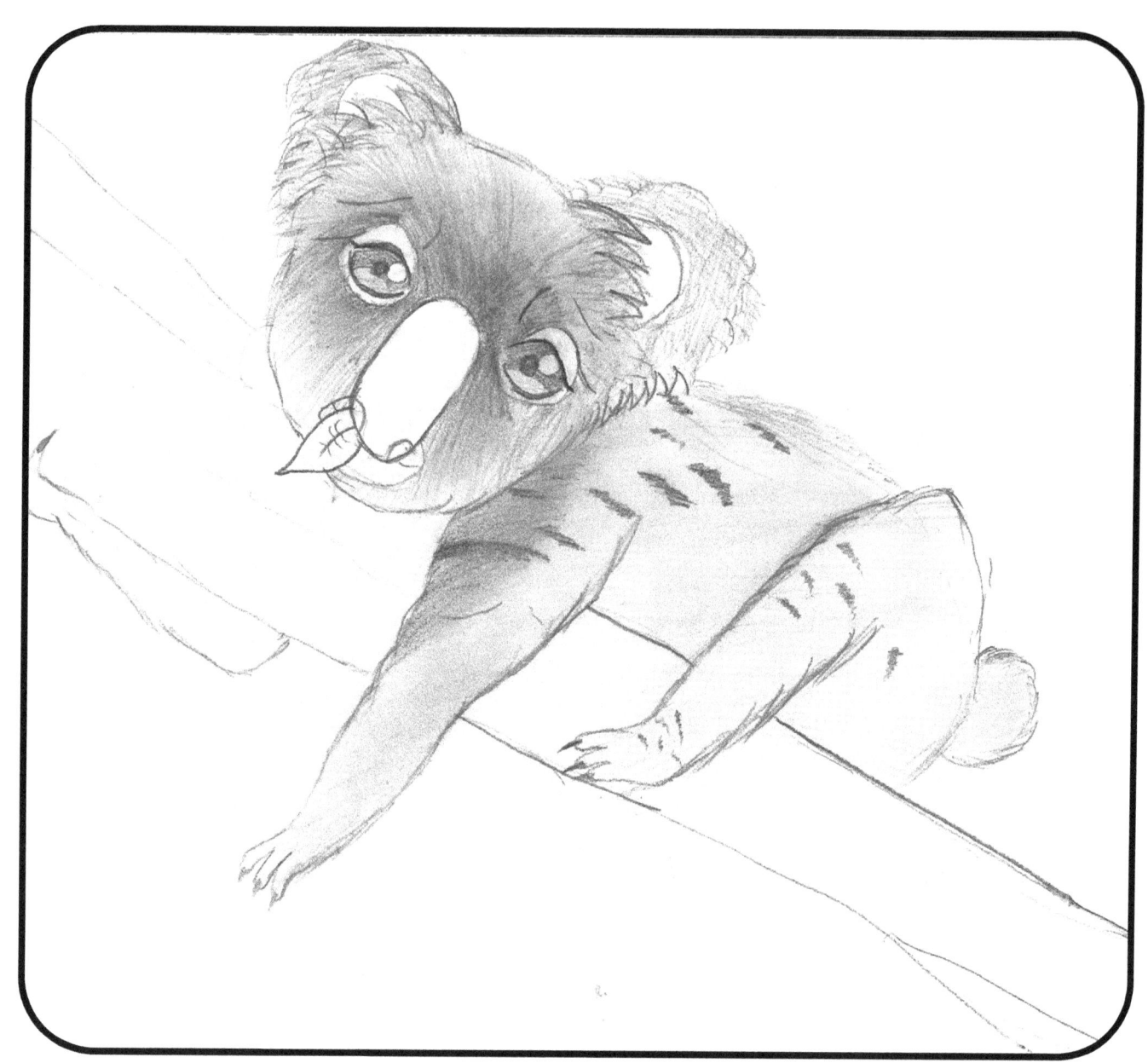

Ailany Morales

**The Koala Bear
likes to sit and eat
even in
the Australian heat**

Julian Meza Morales

The Mockingbird will mock you
all over town
and he won't even stop
when the sun goes down

Julian Meza Morales

The Egyptian Uromastyx
is cold blooded, true
but he's enthusiastics
about meeting me and you

Mlranda Marquez

The Beaver uses
his teeth and tail
to build a dam
that will not fail

Viandi Campos

The Trumpeter Swan
so very proud
of his trumpet
so very loud

Camila Garcia

The Two Toed Sloth
sleeps in a tree
and she'll never fall out
it seems to me

Alondra Rangel

The Kingbird thinks
he's big as an eagle
he may be small
but oh so regal

Ericka Uribe

At night The Coyote
howls at the moon
to me it sounds like
a pretty sweet tune

Miranda Marquez

The Texas Armadillo
lives in a shell
made of his skin I guess
but I really can't tell

Miranda Marquez

The Prairie Dog
is a little chunky
but even so
he's mighty spunky

Natalee Arrieta

The Falcon
likes to dive at 185
and when she flies that fast
she's unsurpassed

Miranda Marquez

The California Condor
soars ever higher
that's because
he's an awesome flyer

Sophia Cortez

The Carolina Chickadee
may be very small
but when she sings
her voice is heard by all

Yaretzi Rojo and Luna Arzate

The Eel is electric
his skin crackles blue
don't swim near him
or he might shock you

Julian Meza Morales

The American Bison
also called a Buffalo
lives on the Great Plains
at least he used to I know

The Toucan sings
a happy song

Miranda Marquez

with her beak
so big and strong

Toucans

Arieanna Escobedo

Estefania Sosa

Juan Hernandez

Bella Moresi

**Brian Cruz
and Carlos Bautista Mendez**

Jacqueline Orozco

Mario Cortez

Richard Moran

Ericka Uribe

Miranda Marquez

The Chipmunk searches
the ground for food
and he's always in
a happy mood

Fatima Ramirez

The Jackrabbit has
long ears and feet
introduce yourself
if by chance you meet

Miranda Marquez

The Nutcracker lives
high up on the slopes
and cracks a lot of nuts there
at least, she hopes

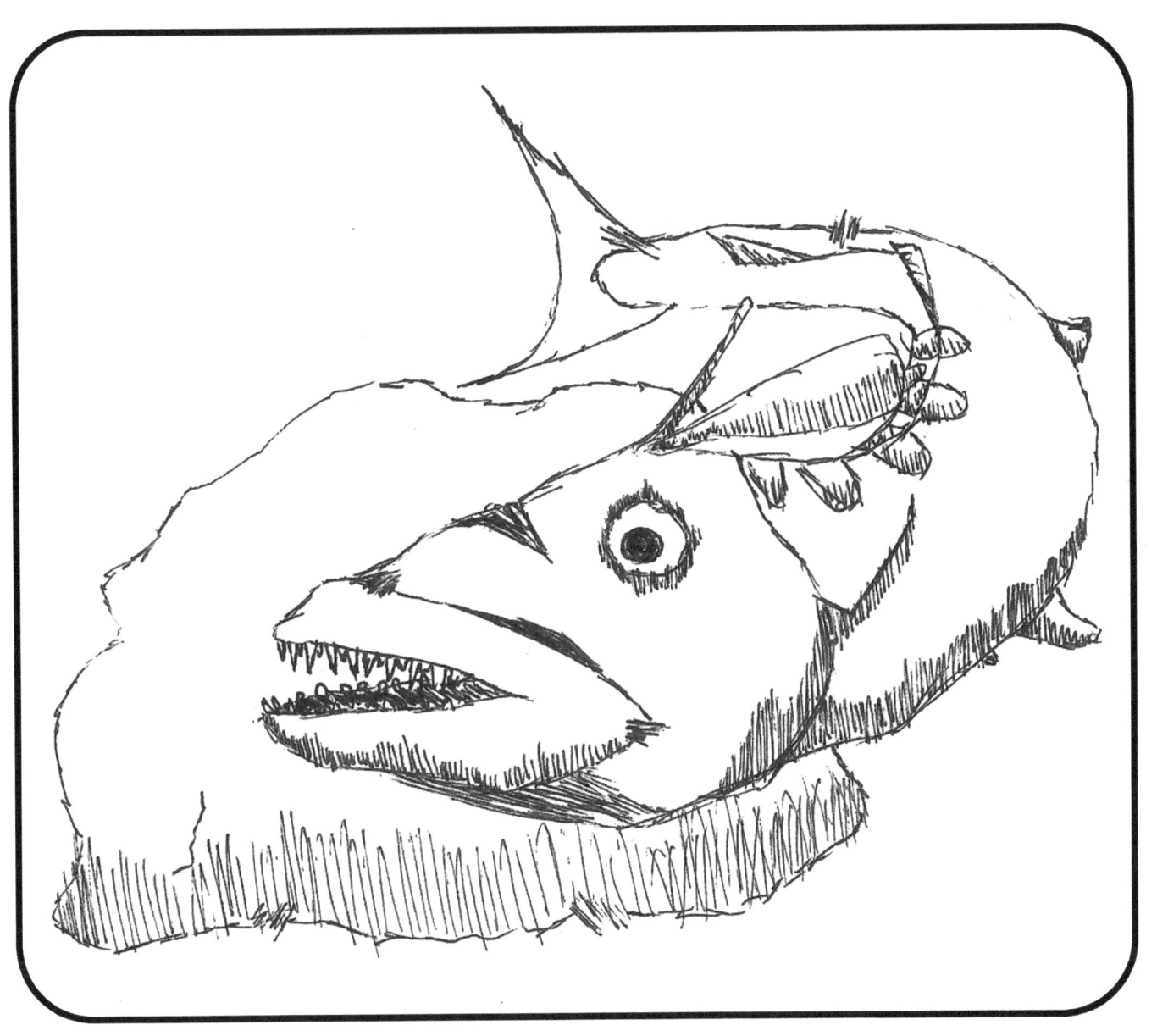

Andres Ulloa

The Barracuda swims
in the deep blue sea
and hides in the rocks
best let her be

Yaretzi Hernandez

The Common Mole
digs real hard
so he can live in a hole
in your backyard

Emily Shearer

The Mink stays warm
in every season
her furry mink coat
is the reason

Bailey Nelson and Angelina Campos

The ears of a Lynx
are pointed, yes
so she can hear everything
more or less

ANONYMOUS

The Long Tailed Weasel
prefers the night
so he can hide
away from the light

Miranda Marquez

The Marmot squeaks
a lonely note
high up in the mountains
his song is wrote

Miranda Marquez

Paedophryne Amauensis
is hard to rhyme
it's just a tiny frog
with a name sublime

Miranda Marquez

The Caiman has a membrane
that nictitates
to better, underwater,
see her dates

Dayanna Melgar

The Rainbow Trout
likes to swim
and he is a fish
so that suits him

The Penguin wears
a feathery tuxedo

Angela Navarro

which if you think about it
is pretty neat-o

Alondra Rangel

The Vermilion Flycatcher
catches lots of flies
but it's really his color
that catches your eyes

Gonzalo Castaneda

The Mollusk will undulate
under the sea
and if you are there to see it
it's the place to be

DO IT YOURSELF

Rhinoceros

_____

_____

_____

_____

DO IT YOURSELF

Duckbill Platypus

_____

_____

_____

_____

DO IT YOURSELF

Ladybug

_____

_____

_____

_____

DO IT YOURSELF

Tarantula

_____

_____

_____

_____

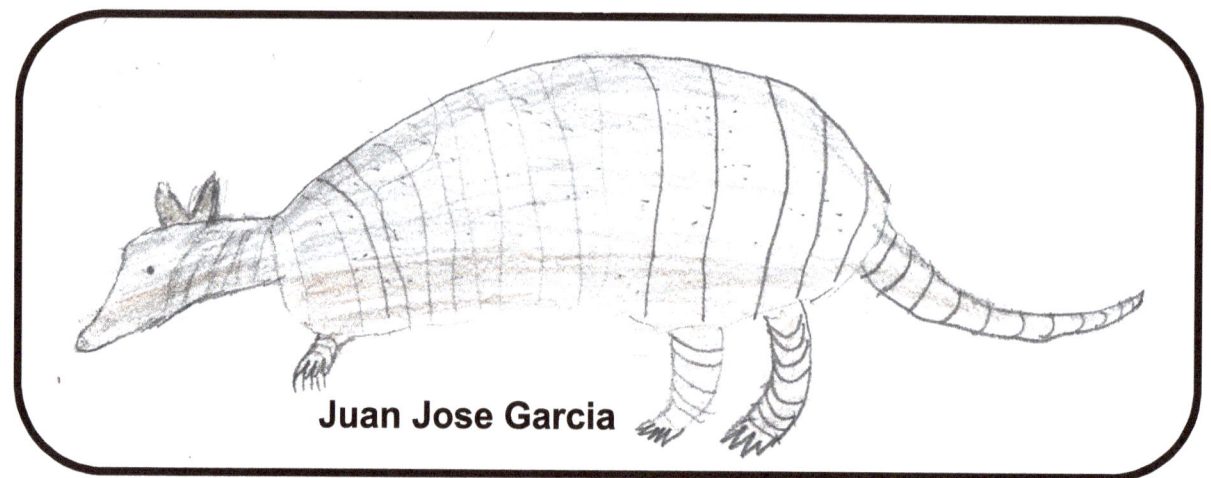

Juan Jose Garcia

Dilver Ramirez and Osvaldo Garcia

Sophia Cortez

Hugo Gutierrez

Alejandra Flores

Miranda Marquez

Julian Meza Morales

Zachary Vance

Evelyn Garcia

Miranda Marquez

Lola and Galilea Jimenez

Edliverto

Jason Martinez Diaz

Damian Vazquez

Jazmin

Leonardo Lomeli

Matthew Franz

Diego Padilla

Bella Moresi

Abigail Vazquez

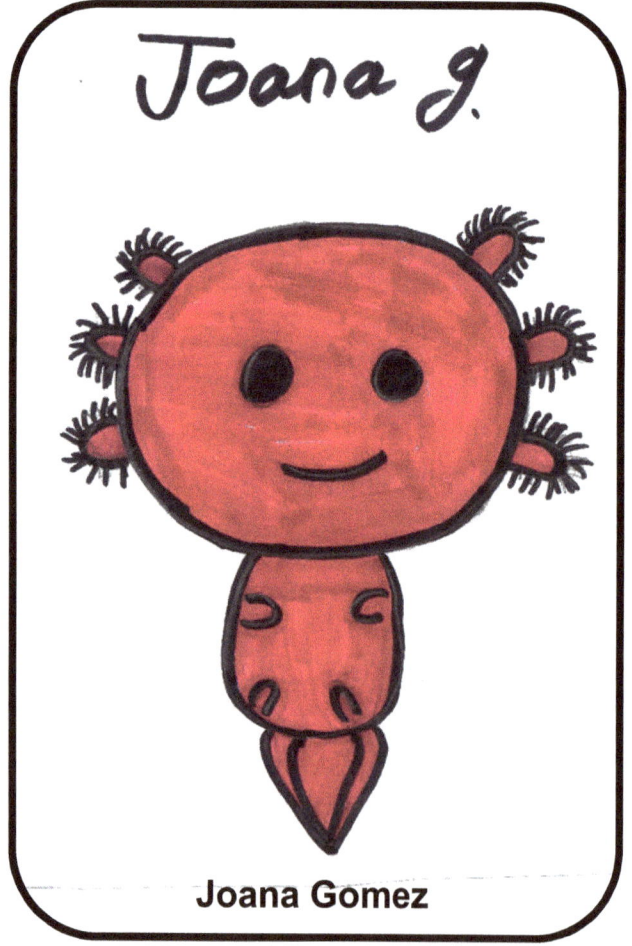

Joana g.

Joana Gomez

Leila

Nuts

Galilea Jimenez

Eden Salas

Cielo Arzate

Fatima Ramirez

Monserrat Martinez Lopez

Erich Ceana Lacbay

Estefania Sosa

Yesenia Soto

Ericka Uribe

Miranda Marquez

Miranda Marquez

Edaim

Marcus Lemus

Alondra Rangel

Bryan Rubio

Luis Aldo

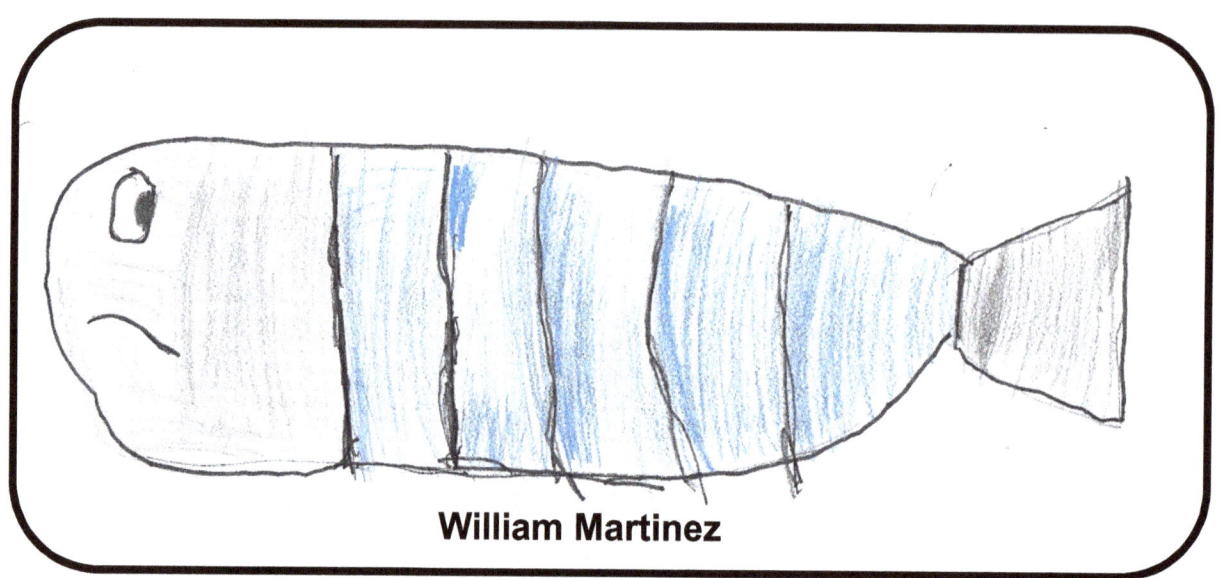

William Martinez

Santiago Lopez

Matthew Franz

Richard Moran

Julieann Rivera

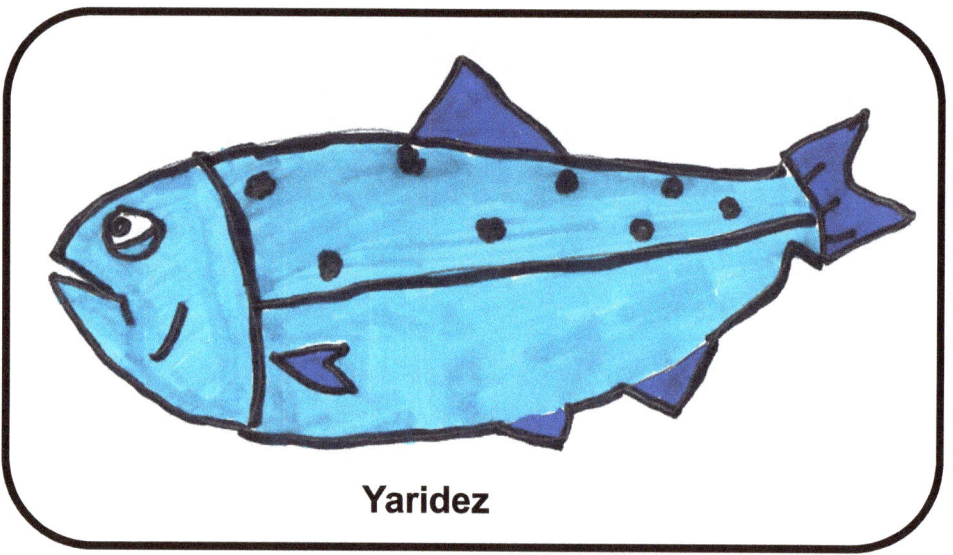

Yaridez

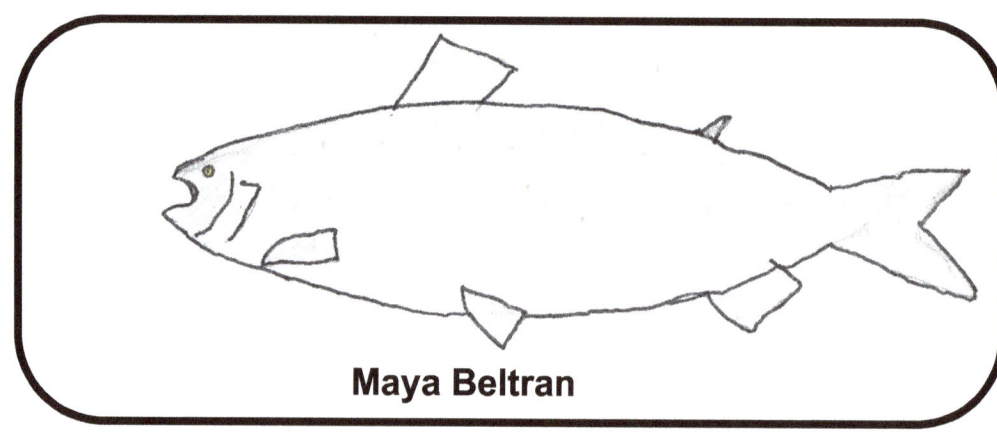

Maya Beltran

Ismael Deras and David

Hugo Gutierrez and Scarlett Keddrick

Isavela Arechiga

Bernice Villa and Sol Arzate

Camila Jimenez

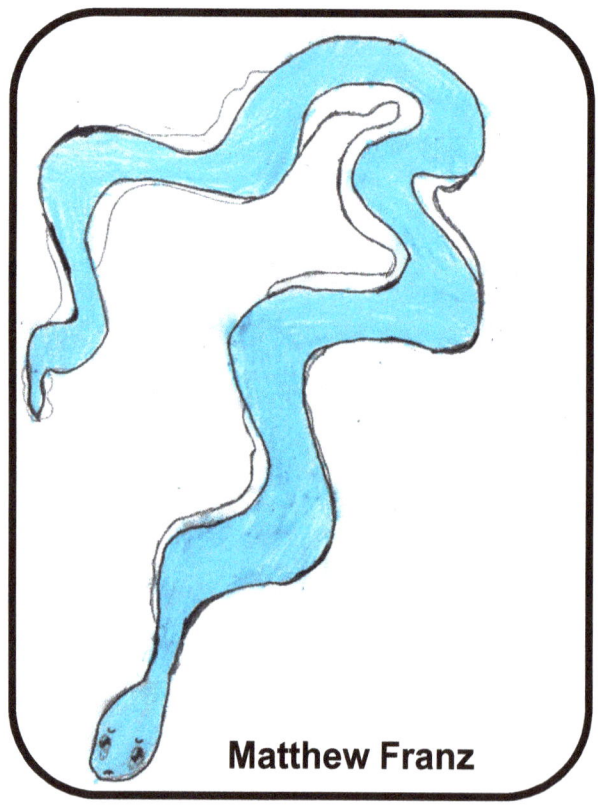

Matthew Franz

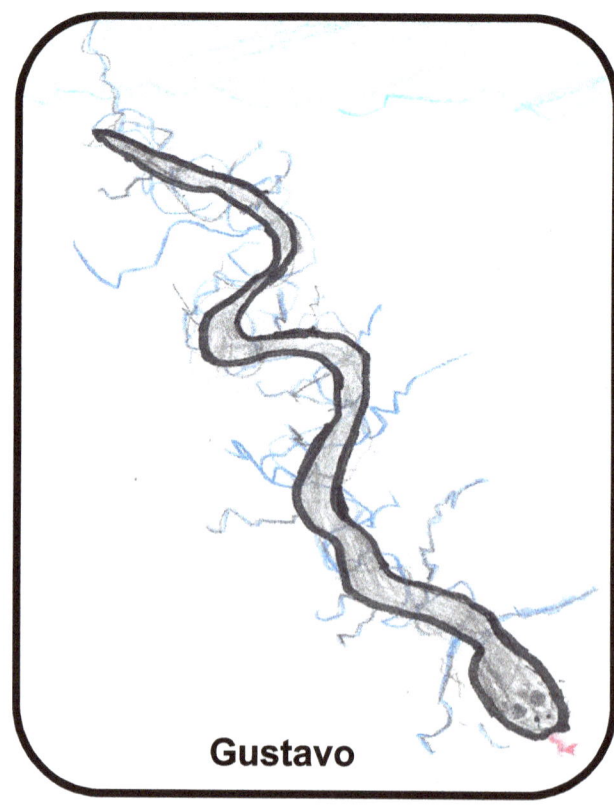

Gustavo

Angelina Campos

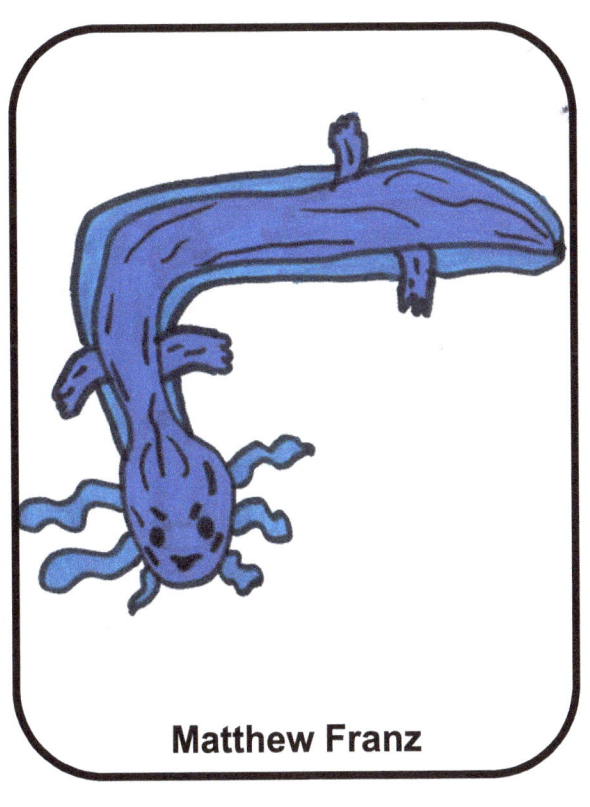

Matthew Franz

David Posada

THE END

ABOUT THE AUTHOR

Rusty Austin began his career writing book and movie reviews at his community college newspaper, The Rapp Street Journal, where he eventually became editor in chief. He moved on to graduate from UCLA Film School and then to Hollywood where he worked for many years as a TV producer. Along the way he discovered a talent for writing poetry. As his Hollywood career wound down he wrote a series of Facebook posts which gradually morphed into a large number of kid friendly and adult savvy poems. He has always had a soft spot for animals and food, so that's what he writes poems about! At the urging of his Facebook family, he turned those posts into books. His books always include a short DIY section to encourage kids to write their own poems and draw their own animals or favorite foods.

Also by Rusty
The Two-Headed Snake
The Unicorn Has One Horn
Beware the Grizzly Bear
The Carrot Is Orange

Alejandra Flores